Shattered Light

Ashley Davis

Dedication

Here's to hoping that my fractured glass can add some color and light to the world.

All made possible by the love of Jesus.

Preface

We have a calling.
Share the light.
We do it through who we are, how we love, and the way
we live.

We are broken people. Restored by a great Light.

Acknowledgements

I'm so grateful for my Savior and the gifts of this life. Some beautiful and some heavy. All teachers.

Thank you, Kyle. My husband and the leader of our little family. Thank you to my boys. I hope to help you scatter light far into the future!

1. Vision

My vision is broken
Fractured like a mirror
And like a mirror, reflects mostly my own brokenness.

The hope is to see the world as You see it.

I'm handcuffed to my own eyes.

I choose the lenses
Sometimes they are chosen for me - beyond my control.

I want to choose Your eyes.
I'm desperate for new ones.

All I see is through the fractures of all I've ever seen

And myself

But you see me, too.

2. Arizona

You can provide shelter, shade, and even protection.
But only when the time is right.

Only when everything lines up.

If I get too close I know you'll hurt me.
Defense to keep yourself safe.

That danger is always there - keeping me just far enough
away.

You hold what I need, but I'll never get it from you until
you are broken.
Until you are broken you will always use your defense.

You like the desert. It's familiar.
You, like the desert, are familiar.

3. Outside as Within

You cannot create outside of you what you don't first create inside of you.

We are a broken people because WE are broken people.

But in me is something greater than me.

Something whole.
Something healing.
Pure love.

I am called It's dwelling place
& If it's in me it can come from me.
Without striving to make it happen.
If I can let go, it would be set free.

It's outside of my control so I open my hands and release the same grace that makes it possible in the first place.

4. Paradox

Fierce and majestic.

Beautiful but mourning.

Ruler.
Good

All powerful and of many sorrows.

Wise King.

Gentle and humble.

Fragile but imperative.

Precious.
Approachable.

All encompassing and of many sorrows.

5. The Most Important Role

They arrive bursting
our hearts open with love than never existed within us
before.

Perfect and fragile.
Moldable but already whole.
Unblemished. Open- to life and to love.

The greatest gift leads us to the most important job.
An impossible role to perfect.

They need us to help them remain perfect and open to
life and to love.

but

6. Calling

We are broken people
living in a broken world

& tasked with loving others and honoring Jesus.

The most difficult call.

Hurting hearts pouring out the love we've been shown-
but from broken vessels. Jars of clay.

Filled with pure gold and making a beautiful, yet
expensive, mess.

Fields of light and energy
fractured by the past.

Wanting nothing more than to allow our nature to take
over.
To radiate and reflect what we are honored to hold.

but limited by our shattered being, we reflect shattered
light.

7. Voices

There are voices left unheard.
Unable to speak out for themselves.

Those hurting and in need of someone. A spokesperson.
Willing to shout what they cannot.

We are told to say something when we see something.
Yet, we see it all around us.
Those with the power to change what we see do not
want to hear anything.

Distracted by what is in front of us.
Looking through a fog we have chosen and ignoring the
great need we persist.

So we close our eyes and listen. Ignore the screaming
distractions.

We can hear the cries for help. We know within us what
we need to do.

Kneel down and reach out.
They are depending on us.

8. Why Did it Take You So Long?

In chains, a slave.
A reality too painful for most people to consider.
Broken repeatedly.
Hopeless and alone, but for the captors and the customers.
She's never known love, only an act that is supposed to be a part of it.
Desperate for light in the darkness.
The only hope she has is death. The only way she sees out.

But, then. Someone comes.
Light carriers.

Free and yet still in bondage. She hears about the Great Love. His sacrifice. His Name.

In tears she wonders -

If He is so good and you all have known His love and redemption - what took you so long?

9. Filled but Empty

She had a great responsibility. More than one but all the same.

She failed.
The broken things in her past prevented her from fulfilling her duties.
She tried to do it. Knew it mattered. Acted it out. But it was all empty.

Hurting and distracted by that hurt. Choosing more pain instead of healing. Choosing anything but what she had.

Bitter and angry. Resentful of what her tasks prevented her from seeking.
Pouring into them all of her hurt, all of her anger, all of her disappointment.

along with tiny bits of hope. Hope that grew with the Love that is beyond her.

We choose to be free from this cycle.
Choose to lay down the hurt passed on to us.
Anger
Bitterness

Disappointment
Pain
Resentment

It can be our legacy.
It's our choice.

10. Grounded

Put here on purpose.
Full of something rare, beautiful, powerful.

Left to the elements.

Worn by the wind.
Washed in the water.
Refined by the friction.
Fractured by the cold.

Steadfast.

& now

Small and smooth. Easily picked up, carried, held, and
cherished.

They say it's just a normal rock-
but aren't we all.

11. Rise and Set

Each new day,
full of hope and promise.

The beauty of fresh mercy.
The energy in ripe opportunity.

What will it hold?

The sun inches up from the horizon.
Not in a whisper or a gentle invitation.

Shouts of color to remind us-

This is it! Today is the day!
Don't miss it.

& then each new night,
full of what you put in.

The sinking sun echoing all that we gave today.

12. Twin Dimensions

Connected on a different level.
We are two dandelions.

Communicating in our own energy but living in the
weeds.

Bringing the joy that rarely only children discover.
Beauty and presence in the mundane.

We thrive in the heat of life. Pushing through and
persisting.
Strong.
Healing.
Useful.
Beautiful.

We are those that carry the light.
Brightness that is made stronger when we are together.
Yet we shine where we are. Too far apart, but still
connected.

On a different level.

13. Crossing Paths

Two travelers.

Each on their own journey,
so grateful to walk on paths that cross.

Collecting the wisdom and love and pain along the way -
We come together and honor the adventure the other has
known.

Understanding what it costs a traveler to collect these
treasures along the way.

Some we have wanted to put down. They are too heavy a
burden to carry for long.

Yet somehow we knew-
If we could get to one another it would be worth it.

We share the strength we developed as we carried the
too heavy things.

14. Broken glass

Anger is responsible for the broken glass.
Innocence is responsible for picking it up.

Because if the task isn't completed, the danger will
remain.

& so

Tender-footed we tiptoe through the shards. Retrieving
the pieces one by one.

The slivers, some too small to see, break skin.
Wounds required of the objective.

The glass is mostly gone now. Not visible to the ones that
didn't know it was there.
But the pain persists.

15. Fragments

The light is strong. Bright and beautiful.

And we, it's carriers.

The light, it pierces. Radiates and shines.

And our path, made safe by it.

The light is heavy. Enormous and important.
Our people, they need it.

The light comes through us. Broken as we are.
A coleidescope of color, made possible by the fractures.

16. Piece of a Puzzle

Some puzzles are made of hundreds of pieces. All the same shape and similar colors.

Some puzzles are made of pieces that are predictable. Coming together in an expected way.

This piece is different.

It doesn't behave like the others. It fits in an unpredictable and unexpected way.

It's unique and funny. Perfectly imperfect. And the puzzle isn't complete without it.

17. Great Sadness

Burdened, even before this life has burdened it.

A great and deep sadness that existed before any sadness
was ever truly known.

Carrier of the grief we will all come to know.
A reflection of the Man of many sorrows.

Tormented by nightmares that most cannot comprehend.

Tears from a place we do not know.

We comfort those who mourn without understanding
the source.

18. Creator

As the created, we create.
Pouring out what is within us.

We want to create something beautiful but is there
beauty within us?

We hope it will be something memorable and important,
but do we carry that?

We attempt to produce something life-giving, something
expansive and worthy.
Do we know that's who we are?

As it is within us, so it will be.

As we acknowledge the Greatness we carry, we can be
responsible for bringing the masterpiece only made
possible by the Master.

www.ingramcontent.com/pod-product-compliance
Lightning Source LLC
La Vergne TN
LVHW050302200726
843509LV00015B/3123